THE FOUND POETRY REVIEW

VOLUME 4: SPRING / SUMMER 2012

MASTHEAD

EDITOR-IN-CHIEF
Jenni B. Baker

SENIOR POETRY EDITOR
Beth Ayer

POETRY EDITORS
Zachary Donisch, Ann Insley, Andy Thompson

COVER PHOTOGRAPH
Gabriella Corrado

ABOUT

THE FOUND POETRY REVIEW celebrates the poetry in the existing and everyday, and is published twice a year. Submit your centos, blackout poems, erasure pieces and other found poems by June 30 for consideration in the spring/summer issue and by December 31 for the fall/winter issue. http://foundpoetryreview.submishmash.com

The Found Poetry Review adheres to the American University Center for Social Media's *Code of Best Practices in Fair Use for Poetry* principle on "found material" which suggests:

> *Under fair use, a poet may make use of quotations from existing poetry, literary prose, and non-literary material, if these quotations are re-presented in poetic forms that add value through significant imaginative or intellectual transformation, whether direct or (as in the case of poetry-generating software) indirect.*

For more details, visit: http://www.centerforsocialmedia.org/fair-use/related-materials/codes/code-best-practices-fair-use-poetry

EMAIL: editor@foundpoetryreview.com
WEBSITE: http://www.foundpoetryreview.com
TWITTER: http://twitter.com/foundpoetryrev
FACEBOOK: http://www.facebook.com/FoundPoetryReview

© 2012, Found Poetry Review. Rights revert to the author upon publication.

CONTENTS

7	**THE MAN WHO TASTES THROUGH LIFE** Danielle Jones-Pruett	
8	**FROM *A NUMBER OF HINTS OR CONCISE LESSONS FOR THE IMPROVEMENT OF YOUTH ON ALL OCCASIONS IN LIFE* (1931)** Danielle Jones-Pruett	
9	**FARM STOCK AND TOOLS AT AUCTION** Danielle Jones-Pruett	
10	**HOLLYWOOD ENDING** Mary Bast	
11	**(THERE) WHERE THE WAVES SHATTER** Margo Roby	
12	**SURROUNDED BY SEAWATER ON A DAILY BASIS** Winston Plowes	
14	**THE SKIN IS NOT JUST SKIN** Jennifer Saunders	
16	**THE EXPAT AT THE CROSSROADS** Jennifer Saunders	
18	**THE HEART IS A PUMP** Annabel Banks	
19	**SKIN** Andrea M. Lockett	
20	**LEADING YOUR ONE-EYED SISTER THROUGH THE NIGHT** John Paul Calavitta	
21	**THE MOMENT BEFORE HISTORY BEGINS** John Paul Calavitta	

22 SIMPLETON WITH A BOMB I HID SHIVERING
    John Paul Calavitta

23 SENSE IS SUCTION FOUNTAINS
    John Paul Calavitta

24 THE BEST ENDEMIC BIRDS
    Nathalie Boisard-Beudin

25 APHASIA LECTURE
    Kristen Shaw

26 ROUNDABOUT LOVE
    Paul Hostovsky

28 ARLENE
    Douglas William Garcia Mowbray

29 DANCING
    Douglas William Garcia Mowbray

30 HELEN KELLER GOES MYSTICAL
    Angela Kirby

31 TEN THINGS EVERYONE SHOULD KNOW ABOUT TIME
    Angela Kirby

32 FOR JANE KENYON, IN THE DARK
    Deborah Hauser

33 THIS IS HOW SALVATION FINDS YOU
    Deborah Hauser

34 ERASING BOUNDARIES
    Chris Cannella

36 TAKE IT AWAY
    Angela Croft

37 ROAD SIGNS
    Deborah Dungan

38	**MY TEST** David Elzey
40	**THE OLD MEN AT THE ZOO** Cathryn Andresen
41	**AESOP'S MANAGEMENT FABLES** Cathryn Andresen
42	**COLLAGE II (GIFTS)** Monica Wendel
43	**COLLAGE IV (HUMBOLDT STREET)** Monica Wendel
44	**COMPROMISED** Maria Cohut
45	**BABY SHOES, NEVER WORN** Joyce Peseroff
46	**CONTRIBUTORS**

THE MAN WHO TASTES THROUGH LIFE

DANIELLE JONES-PRUETT

synesthesia, n.: a subjective sensation of a sense other than the one being stimulated.

My name, James, is sliced apples. I live in a two-story townhouse, mashed potatoes, a fruit gum block. The neighbors leaving for church are yogurt and jellybeans, just a touch canning wax. I've dated fluffy egg whites, tinned tomatoes, raisins hard from the cellar. The only girl I've ever loved, milk. It spoiled. I still remember granny's lap — pear drops, furniture polish, the sleeve of my favorite train pajamas, chewed into the night.

SOURCE: Statements compiled from J I Wannerton's website (http://www.jwannerton.pwp.blueyonder.co.uk/index1.htm)

FROM *A NUMBER OF HINTS OR CONCISE LESSONS FOR THE IMPROVEMENT OF YOUTH ON ALL OCCASIONS IN LIFE* (1931)

DANIELLE JONES-PRUETT

Study dignity of manners. Don't talk too loud, or much.
Be modest and moderate. Avoid everything masculine.
Don't even hear a double entendre. Never forget to blush.

Dare to be prudish! Receive salutes modestly.
Don't boast of your strengths. Forget about trends.
Study dignity of manners. Don't talk too loud, or much.

Be cautious when dancing, be not too free,
but always be friendly with men.
Don't even hear a double entendre. Never forget to blush.

Don't read novels: let your study be history.
Men cannot be your friends.
Study dignity of manners. Don't talk too loud. Or much.

Be discreet. Avoid all intimacy.
Best not to let love begin.
Don't even hear a double entendre. Never forget to blush.

In both love and war, one needs a strategy.
If you must go to a play, make it a tragedy.
Study dignity of manners. Don't talk too loud or much.
Don't even hear a double entendre. Never forget to blush.

SOURCE: The book *The Honours of the Table or, Rules for Behaviour during Meals; with the Whole Art of Carving* (1931)

FARM STOCK AND TOOLS AT AUCTION

DANIELLE JONES-PRUETT

Felton House: Peabody, Massachusetts

The subscriber being about to make a change

in his business, will sell at auction, on Thursday, April 24th, at One O'clock, P.M., at his farm

on Felton Street, Peabody, the following personal property:

one black horse, 6 years old, sound and kind and a good traveller; one Bay Horse, three cows, one 2 year old

Heifer; a lot of fowls; one Carryall; one side-spring wagon

with two seats; two Express harnesses; one Ox Cart; one Horse Cart; one Plough; Rakes; Hoes;

Lots of land.

SOURCE: Auction poster (circa 19th Century) at the Felton Historic House at Brooksby Farm in Peabody, Massachusetts

HOLLYWOOD ENDING

MARY BAST

I want to write poetry with panache,
brilliant and bawdy prose,
show exceptional taste,
eat Hersheys in the park,

be fluent in flowers, indulge
in Latin leanings, jazz
sensibilities, create a sound
that changes everything for me.

But the chasm between *mi casa*
and *su casa* confounds my life:
are these proving grounds
or the devil's workshop?

Butt out, I said yesterday.
Now I sit in a booth,
decide between a small umbrella
and an olive on a sword.

Orphaned, I will book a room
a world away with soaring windows,
wait for the miracle I feel but never see,
read the silence of the educated fans.

SOURCE: Articles in *The New Yorker* (May 6, 2002)

(THERE) WHERE THE WAVES SHATTER

MARGO ROBY

In the wave-strike over unquiet stones I am nothing
but the empty net which has gone on ahead;
everything comes from your extinguished life
and returns — eternal — to being and nothingness.

It is the hour of departure, the hard cold hour.
The night wind turns in the sky and sings:
it is the tongue of death looking for the dead
in the wave-strike over unquiet stones.

While the blue night dropped on the world,
lapping the ground in search of the dead,
to whoever is not listening to the sea, I am nothing
but the empty net which has gone on ahead.

The sea destroys its continual forms, collapses
its turrets of wildness and whiteness in me;
nothing is extinguished or forgotten:
everything comes from your extinguished life.

Our lives return to the wall, to the rocks of the sea
and the sea is beating, dying and continuing:
ay, love is a journey through water and stars
and returns, eternal, to being and nothingness.

SOURCES: Pablo Neruda's poems "Carnal Apple," "In the Wave-strike," "A Song of Despair," "Chant to Bolivar," "Clenched Soul," "Death Alone," "Enigmas," "20 Poems," "If You Forget," "Love, We're Going Home Now," "Poet's Obligation" and "Sonnet IX"

SURROUNDED BY SEAWATER ON A DAILY BASIS

WINSTON PLOWES

Muck (*Eilean nam Muc*) 30
Bruray 26
Papa Stour 23
Rùm 22
Graemsay 21
Grimsay (South) (*Griomasaigh*) 19
Wyre 18
Ulva (*Ulbha*) 16
Inchmurrin (*Innis Mheadhran*) 13
Holy Isle (*Eilean MoLaise*) 13
Isle of Ewe (*Eilean Iùbh*) 12
Flodaigh 11
Scalpay (*Sgalpaigh*) 10
Papa Stronsay 10
Eilean Shona 9
Erraid (*Eilean Earraid*) 8
Soay (*Sòdhaigh*) 7
Lunga 7
Sanday (*Sandaigh*) 6
Canna (*Eilean Chanaigh*) 6
Tanera Mòr (*Tannara Mòr*) 5
Oronsay (*Orasaigh*) 5
Gometra (*Gòmastra*) 5
Danna 5
Auskerry 5
Moncrieffe Island (*Eilean Monadh Craoibhe*) 3
Inchtavannach (*Innis Taigh a' Mhanaich*) 3
Gairsay 3
Vaila 2
South Rona (*Rònaigh*) 2
Inchfad (*Innis Fada*) 2
Inchcolm (*Innis Choluim*) 2
Eilean Bàn, Lochalsh 2
Davaar (*Eilean Dà Bhàrr*) 2
Shuna (*Siuna*) 1
Sanda Island (*Sandaigh*) 1

Eilean Donan 1
Innis Chonan 1
Fraoch-eilean Unknown

SOURCE: Wikipedia article *Lists of Islands of Scotland*, which draws its data from The General Register Office for Scotland (28 November 2003) *Occasional Paper No 10: Statistics for Inhabited Islands*

THE SKIN IS NOT JUST SKIN

JENNIFER SAUNDERS

This story tells itself as it grows.
How our bodies took notice one of the other —
the pulled bow teasing, pleading.
A first moment of touch.
The thing not yet given
already then inevitable.

The first time I tasted you I thought:
I don't know anything anymore.
Finding the way through the dark,
carrying laundry, washing the windows, straightening up
as if nothing had happened.

The second time I tasted you I thought:
June strawberries.
And the newness after that, and newness again,
the litter of blue-gold,
of air and silver and oh God you.

When did we drift into each other's arms,
nudging each other blindly in the brilliant dark?
I open like a poppy
in your hand and the answer is yes.

SOURCES:

Anita Skeen "What the Seed Knows"

Marge Piercy, "The place where everything changed"
Arielle Greenberg, "On Bodily Love"
Kennette Wilkes, "Dolce"
Alan Yount, "Sharing"
Dorianne Laux, "Balance"
Jane Hirshfield, "Balance"

Marge Piercy, "The first time I tasted you"
Adrie Kusserow, "Thirty-One, Anthropologist, No Gods Left"
Patti Tana, "The River"
Jane Hirshfield, "The Silence"
Dorianne Laux, "After Twelve Days of Rain"

Marge Piercy, "The first time I tasted you"
Susan Rich, "In the Beginning"
Jack Gilbert, "The Spirit and the Soul"
Susan Rich, "Letter to the End of the Year"
Sarah Vap, "Night"

David Baker, "Envoi: Waking After Snow"
Jack Gilbert, "Moment of Grace"
Adrie Kusserow, "Night Poppies"
Traci Brimhall, "The Light in the Basement"

THE EXPAT AT THE CROSSROADS

JENNIFER SAUNDERS

You change a life
with salvaged alphabets and song,
disappearing one country for the next
and wanting the world.
You could start your life over, sitting here,
prepared with a satchel packed, a suitcase,
looking always ahead.

What to do?
To stay in the odd intersections
hinged between worlds,
rules flung across the lost luggage of border crossings?
A legend of broken maps,
the small truths and shaded relief —
choices pondered but not finally taken.
A person, too, holds her lines of possible fracture.

But the tightrope of a life asks more:
given up to the motion of backward, forward,
the invisible boundary line
no longer exists.
Left foot? Yes. Right foot? Yes.
Only between do we walk with determined purpose.

SOURCES:

Jane Hirshfield "To Judgment: An Assay"
Susan Rich, "Nocturn"
Susan Rich, "The Exile Reconsiders"
Susan Rich "The Mapparium"
Susan Rich ""At the Corner of Washington and Third"
Susan Rich "What You Americans Should Know: Partial Stories"
Jane Hirshfield "Each Step"

Jane Hirshfield "A Day Comes"
Susan Rich "The Filigree of the Familiar"
Jane Hirshfield "The Door"
Susan Rich "Mr. Saturday Night"
Susan Rich "The Exile Reconsiders"
Susan Rich "How to Read a Map"
Jane Hirshfield "Vilnius"
Jane Hirshfield "Jasper, Feldspar, Quartzite"

Susan Rich "Until This Evening"
Susan Rich, "Nisqually 6.8"
Susan Rich "Bosnia, Again"
Susan Rich "Iska's Story"
Jane Hirshfield "'It is Night. It is Very Dark.'"
Jane Hirshfield "What Falls"

THE HEART IS A PUMP

ANNABEL BANKS

and a great source of terror to commercial men
(it was clear no help was to be looked for in that quarter)

yet I am accustomed to various experiments. It will be thus observed
the hissing, fiery little machine continues to correspond

despite imperfect mechanical manufacture of the day
three way cock, slide valves and valve clacks. Study the fire engine,

some enabled model capable of executing this race, the double
vessel with advocate beat. I could supply him with dolls' eyes,

this disgraceful state of the coinage. It's a subject I cannot speak
    to him
about. He ought to come hither, the proposed partnership,

the infusion of young blood with power and majesty. Order,
despatch, and the appetite for knowledge. More, I do not
    violently desire.

SOURCE: *Lives of Boulton and Watt* by Samuel Smiles (1865)

SKIN

ANDREA M. LOCKETT

Skin is the edge
to which nerves run their finest feelers.

It throws a seductive curve
over the tragus of the ear;
its creases coalesce on the knuckles
like knots on a pine board.

Soft and stretched, it plays
a medley of textures across the body's contours —
shiny, baggy, freckled, pimply, plump —
shrinks back from cool new touch,
blushes up with fear or fever.

Only this flimsy bit of dermis
separates the vastness of the cosmos
from the rush of blood and conscience that is you.

Skin is a seam shot through with holes — nostrils, pores, and sockets.
To be alive, you must let things in and out:
oxygen and sunlight, the smell of fresh baked bread,
things that nibble, pierce, abrade, and sear.

This organ is a border that protects
but does not hold the world at bay:
Within its margins — you,
beyond its flexy surface—everything.

SOURCE: "Identity's Edge" by Andrea Jones, in *Orion* Magazine, January/February 2007

LEADING YOUR ONE-EYED SISTER THROUGH THE NIGHT

JOHN PAUL CALAVITTA

we guide the blindfold creature
from door to door down

down to midnight
casting her chaplet of light

this is a story Jung would understand

SOURCE: Altered first lines from 19th century poems

THE MOMENT BEFORE HISTORY BEGINS

JOHN PAUL CALAVITTA

reminds me of a former moment
the year one thousand

four hundred thirteen
to be exact

this moment of meeting
between chronologies,

in the first year of the last disgrace

SOURCE: Altered first lines from 19th century poems

SIMPLETON WITH A BOMB I HID SHIVERING

JOHN PAUL CALAVITTA

with poems or murders or empires
in my pocket

my love is broken where a hand
rested on the gun,

the broken glasses and the ticking of the gramophone
fill your pockets

SOURCE: Altered first lines from 19th century poems

SENSE IS SUCTION FOUNTAINS

JOHN PAUL CALAVITTA

in some city underneath an occult star

in a real city, bored with dragon
hand-cuffed to a mysterious silo of glass

you kiss someone because a voice said
we are at war

SOURCE: Altered first lines from 19th century poems

THE BEST ENDEMIC BIRDS

NATHALIE BOISARD-BEUDIN

Sorry for being so silent
She died like snow
Who am I kidding? There's no point. None.
The perspectives are gorgeous

Sorry for being so silent
Let's hold hands and disappear
At railway station. Soaked.
You didn't mention any warning.

Sorry for being so silent
It was that blank page, officer.
The whale was already dead when we got there
There's no point. None.

Sorry for being so silent
Meanders are so pretty, so lush, so beguiling
Why aren't we drinking hurricanes?
Look at isotope ratios in the interstellar gas.

Sorry for being so silent
I've compressed my grandmother
Applied physics confusing biology
There's no point.

She died like snow.

SOURCE: Tweets from @birdchick, @KenKaminesky, @iamreddave, @OnlyAnnie, @moscerina, @KenKaminesky, @JillTracymusic, @CherylMorgan, @FlavorofItaly, @KenKaminesky, @MrBillyBones, @scalzi, @OnlyAnnie, @KenKaminesky, @spacedlaw, @bstiteler, @ESAHerschel, @KenKaminesky, @MassimoBottura, @Samosthenurus, @OnlyAnnie, @iamreddave

APHASIA LECTURE

KRISTEN SHAW

You wake up one morning, and all the tools
and all the animals are gone,
but they're not gone. You haven't
lost them. When you hear
a dog bark, you
haven't forgotten
about dog. The dog
isn't lost. It's not about loss.

SOURCE: Guest lecture on neurological cognitive and language disorders delivered by Diane Kendall at the University of Washington on January 3, 2011.

ROUNDABOUT LOVE

PAUL HOSTOVSKY

We lived with Grandmother then.
Because Mother hadn't enough money
to pay for rent and all of that.
It was a house at the intersection of six roads
which all led to the ocean.

The house looked out on a roundabout
like a wheel with six spokes
where the cars and trucks and motorbikes
and all of the bicycles of Manila
took turns turning.

All those wheels turning inside a wheel
put me in mind of a clockwork,
or the clicking cylinders of a safe
or a brain.

I was eleven or twelve, and Jolie
was fifteen or sixteen and very
pretty already. So there was this boy.

He lived across the street.
Across the first of the six streets.
A young Spanish boy in a house with many windows.

Now we didn't know this boy
and he didn't know us. But he liked Jolie.
He could see her from his windows.

We already had a telephone then
because Grandmother needed a phone
to call the doctor or the druggist or her sons.
It was a big black phone that made a clicking
bicycle sound when you dialed it.

Now the boy across the street had a telephone too.
But he had no way of knowing our number.

But he had his windows. And he was determined.
The wheels were turning inside his head.

He worked very hard and for a very long time
dialing all the numbers.
All of the possible combinations,
like he was trying to crack a safe
one phone number at a time,
running to the window each time to listen,
to see if our phone was ringing.

It was one of those crazy great ideas
men get when they're in love.
The kind that just might work.
The kind that makes a man great
and gets him the woman.
It was a crazy great idea.

It took him several months,
but one day he dialed a number
and went to the window and saw Jolie
picking up the phone —

I remember it very well.
She was wearing a red dress
when he introduced himself to her
from across the rotary,
standing in one of his windows,
smiling a big smile into the phone.

His name was Joaquin Galvis.
He and Jolie had several dates after that.
Then they put in a traffic light
and we moved away to Fagayan
to live with my Uncle Jess.

SOURCE: Letter from Maria Pilar Afzelius written to the author in 1985.

ARLENE

DOUGLAS WILLIAM GARCIA MOWBRAY

The other night
my married son
called me up
and asked me
what I made for dinner.

I said:
stuffed peppers —

and he said he'd be right over.

I told him

you have a wife now,
get her to cook for you.

SOURCE: Overheard conversation at work

DANCING

DOUGLAS WILLIAM GARCIA MOWBRAY

oh, i love to dance.

i have a friend named Lauren
and I think she is the danciest person i know.

i don't always want to dance,
but it's kind of like
when you were little and
didn't want to take a bath.

cuz even though
i don't feel like it at first,
once i start it i feel better and
i don't want to stop.

another good thing about dancing
is that i have never seen
a bad dancer in my whole life.

dance!
and if you don't have music
then sing yr own.

SOURCE: Slightly revised version of a student's essay for the Maryland School Assessment

HELEN KELLER GOES MYSTICAL

ANGELA KIRBY

After tribulations inseparable from pleasure, you think of seeing
the nature of God, blind as darkness, not knowing a divine
thing: perhaps brighter companions know the universe
is all a dream, and only the blind are awake. Yes, no: at the last
day of the unseen world, the strange grass and skies are greener,
bluer than ordinary. A thousand things escape from the envious
imagination: it creates stars in cobblestones, realms spread
out like the flash of a blade in its rainbow, the solar system
a suburb of wild desire. Invest in being frivolous as a merry-
go-round on quiet days: pleasant surprise, to satisfy craving
the superlative (demigod/god, highest/largest) — only the most
costly breath is a victory of beasts. From this vantage, the impossible
sees a rival stand luminary in the storm (cynics will say groping
toward sight), weary with the long thoughts that bring happiness.

SOURCE: Letter from Helen Keller to Dr. John Finley, dated January 13, 1932

TEN THINGS EVERYONE SHOULD KNOW ABOUT TIME

ANGELA KIRBY

1. Time might get common, of course — set alarm clocks, organize moments — a different mess, perhaps fundamental. We used to emerge from atoms. Nobody knows for sure.

2. The past isn't completely accepted. Now is in the books, and the future will lie.

3. Everyone is true at the level of biology. Time depends on how the speed of light accumulates memories — we are real when we're older.

4. You live in the past, in one hand. Your nose, your feet are mysterious to your brain. You experience touch as simultaneous, but reconciliation takes time to assemble — the lag between us is about 80 milliseconds.

5. Your memory isn't you. When the past is wrong, you can have the least reliable form.

6. Consciousness depends on manipulating aquatic life. Land-based animals have the origin of grammar to talk about. A future with each other wouldn't be possible without it. Imagine.

7. Disorder increases aging; order is more natural. How account for all the rest?

8. Complexity comes and goes. Between entropy and the ephemeral, life — we're far from complete.

9. Aging can part the universe or build a refrigerator. The arrow of time is a physical impossibility for me.

10. A billion heartbeats die. Sad is necessary. Life pushes out animals with real experience until we become immortal.

SOURCE: "Ten Things Everyone Should Know about Time," *Discover Magazine*. September 1, 2011

FOR JANE KENYON, IN THE DARK

DEBORAH HAUSER

I feel my life moaning on the fire.
The sun bright, if not warm,
does not destroy my sorrow,
but only stirs outlandish sadness.

I cling to ravaged language, to the sacrament
of No. Sleepless, I gather stones to contain
my vanishing. I have been interrogated
for the unquenchable fire.

The wineglass I hold, weary of holding
wine, could have been redeemable. It is not
enough to find my mate in these vast
blue latitudes. It seems like the next thing

to do before I lose my place, but the old comfort
does not rise, the bough does not sway.
Still, I settle, in the dark.

SOURCE: *Collected Poems* of Jane Kenyon

THIS IS HOW SALVATION FINDS YOU

DEBORAH HAUSER

The scissors, once sharpened, inspire
a growing compulsion to cut

my hair, to forget what I know, to stop
whistling for the bird that escaped her cage,

to stop these accidents of inattention.
The dull bread knife feigns indifference, will not

be seduced, refuses translation.
The whiskey is only clouded sky

where the lilacs never bloomed for any one.
There are suddenly windows. Can we endure

it, the rain finally stopped? Slower now.
Can we endure the unrequited

astonishment of starlight falling
onto burning leaves.

SOURCE: *The Good Thief* by Marie Howe

ERASING BOUNDARIES

CHRIS CANNELLA

I

My face in the morning mirror, small bones
breaking through brown skin asking me
to explain broken glass. Can I call anything
mine? I'm worried something will change
while I sleep. I search for skulls and extra
ribs, falling in love with what remains
in the past. Am I the garbage man
of your dreams? I remember buckets
of dirty water at the uranium mine.
I remember waiting for my brother,
wanting to follow him and recover myself again.

II

I recognize the need to prove blood
against blood. We all want to survive—
my father is still running, looking
to find a way home. I give thanks
to the chains (there are places
I can not leave), I give thanks to the whips
(so many illusions I need to believe).
There is a reservation for every
prisoner willing to accept
their four walls and window—
animals formed by the absence of song.

Do I give away what is mine, leaving tracks
in the snow? Hunger becomes madness easily.
I worry the reservation will become
a pox blanket wrapped around our shoulders.

I was frozen between steps forgiving
my inadequate god. Our spirit animals
chased us back between past and present.
Our bodies forget the rhythm of survival.

III

I am an American
Indian and have
learned the word
that determines our
dreams. Sometimes
I am suddenly empty
without hope of rain.
I don't know any
beautiful words for death,
only voices and dreams
distorted by tin speakers.
I wear the color of my
skin like a brown paper
bag wrapped around a bottle.
I give away what is mine
because you have seen
the color of my bare skin.

SOURCE: Sherman Alexie's *Old Shirts & New Skins* (1993)

TAKE IT AWAY

ANGELA CROFT

You can place almost anything between
two slices of bread & butter & call it a sandwich

conceal contents so alluring as to arouse a man's
curiosity, tempt his pallet

the *Ham Sandwich* can be made by mincing
three or four pounds of hock into a paste,

adding mustard & cream or top of the milk
so it will spread easily

& do away with the possibility of biting
into it & finding the filling comes away,

leaving you with two barren pieces of bread
in your hand - the ham hanging out of your mouth

SOURCE: *Popular Catering without Waste* by Christian Brook-Jackson

ROAD SIGNS

DEBORAH DUNGAN

Come ride with me to Shiprock

Past Aztec and Hesparus
Bloomfield and Fruitland

Over the Animas and the La Plata
to Waterflow

We'll shop for pawn and propane
eat kneel down bread
and
foster a future

SOURCE: Road signs and billboards observed on a drive between Santa Fe and Shiprock

MY TEST

DAVID ELZEY

I
tried to rewrite my brain.

The world seemed
wide open
spellbound by
potential,

wonderful and terrifying.
The room started to dis-
integrate
the plaster walls, the
chattering noise, the facial hair of my
compatriots
broke apart.
My senses
were out of control.
The world rushed in relentlessly.

Blocking
information
opens the floodgates
– and that's just what it felt
like. I

was going mad.

The hope of manipulating potential
remained elusive.

That didn't stop
me.
I
watched
the sidewalk
toss, the
surf swell.

I wanted to strip
and let reality enter.

We favor
depression, anxiety,
an extra thick
blanket
of anguish and anxiety,
a solip-
sistic safety zone, protected from too
much reality.

Time
to hunker down and play it safe.

SOURCE: "My Kool Acid Test." *Newsweek*, March 26/April 2, 2012

THE OLD MEN AT THE ZOO

CATHRYN ANDRESEN

From SPINE: The Paperback Centos

the girls of slender means
carnal innocence
great expectations

and they were not ashamed
to love and be loved

then came you
the man without qualities
seven types of ambiguity
double scotch & wry
slow heat in heaven
an error in judgment

nothing sticks like a shadow
three steps behind
once and always
sentimental education
fading echoes
of human bondage

after many a summer dies the swan
a room of one's own
one hundred years of solitude
a handful of dust

all the lonely people
in the company of others

SOURCE: Various book titles

AESOP'S MANAGEMENT FABLES

CATHRYN ANDRESEN

From SPINE: The Paperback Centos

he came to set the captives free
opening up the scriptures
settling accounts

pulling down strongholds
the elephant in my living room
greed and glory on wall street
muting white noise
donkey gospel

dismantling privilege
green mansions
shelters of stones

unended quest
the weary titan
looking forward

he still moves stones
but who will bell the cats

SOURCE: Various book titles

COLLAGE II (GIFTS)

MONICA WENDEL

Shower us with your gifts of bronze
skinned bots and humans holding hands.
We could do wine or poems, too.
I used to work as a pastry baker, but you
were in my dream last night, knocking
around late in the evening, selling tickets
for some Vassar thing. Come, you weeper.
Take from this what you will (but not
the sensitive information).

SOURCE: Personal emails and GChat conversations between Monica Wendel and Elsbeth Pancrazi between March 2012 and April 2012

COLLAGE IV (HUMBOLDT STREET)

MONICA WENDEL

Friends, you divide and bury bulbs
over the winter, just under the surface
of the soil. Although it is far away,
I'm home now, and so many things
remind me of the day we went by the river.
A plan has been hatched. We're keeping
things magical, carefully with slow hands
so as not to bruise, waiting for the ground to break.

SOURCE: Personal emails between Monica Wendel and Elsbeth Pancrazi between July 2011 and April 2012

COMPROMISED

MARIA COHUT

in thus adopting the superstitions of the ancients,
he often went to see her at the hotel —
how moving she is in this centuries-old consumption:
'No, I will not be both held witch and strumpet!'
he was compelled to turn to translation,
there was a laugh among the unfeeling —
she was dead, dead from not having comprehended.

this has been going on for hundreds of years;
a stainless mirror like a bell
had clearly forbidden her to open the door
to some of the ridiculous and indecent tricks
of the Rosicrucian Order – nothing really happens
by chance. she saw herself, now without hope,
the reverse of the Mab or Titania.

even though winter came, spring came,
a dark musty tunnel, so empty, so quiet —
what happened? fierce and funereal delights,
the entire bodies of the factory maidens
were struck with shivers. he recalled
stories of satanism: one can see similarities,
the usual sort of evidence — habit is the law.

SOURCES:
- *VIVO: The Life of Gustav Meyrink*, Mike Mitchell, Dedalus 2008
- *Bruges-la-Morte*, Georges Rodenbach, translation Mike Mitchell & Will Stone, Dedalus 2007
- *Letters on Demonology and Witchcraft*, Sir Walter Scott, Wordsworth Editions 2001
- *Mystery of the Maya*, R.A. Montgomery, Bantam Books 1981
- *The Prose Poem of the Elizabethan Collar*, Kenji Otsuki, in Gothic & Lolita Bible – Winter 2009

BABY SHOES, NEVER WORN

JOYCE PESEROFF

Look what that bitch's selling on eBay!
I spent good money for a pair with lizard trim,
more than her BFF spent on a Stop & Shop turkey
she carved at the shower into bitty slices
as if she'd basted it herself. But didn't
her sister tell me the baby
was born without feet,
and that her blue-eyed Lubavicher rabbi
said, "The purpose of children is to break
your heart," so if you never wept
and want to, have a kid.

SOURCE: Compilation of quotations from student responses to a creative writing lesson prompt

CONTRIBUTORS

CATHRYN ANDRESEN has published three chapbooks and a poetry workbook for young children. "Ditty Bag," her three-dimensional chapbook, was included in *The Art of the Book IV* exhibit at the Artists Union Gallery in Ventura, California. Cathryn is the editor of *Quintessence – an Anthology* (VCWC Press-2008), and her poetry has appeared in *A Bird Black as the Sun* (Green Poet Press 2011) and journals including *ASKEW, Naked Knuckle, Fresh Ink* and *The Advocate.* More at www.cathryn-andresen.com.

ANNABEL BANKS is an English writer in her thirties. She graduated from Cambridge university with a degree in English in 2010, and gained her Creative Writing MA with distinction from Royal Holloway in 2011. She is currently in the first year of her poetry PhD at University College Falmouth. Annabel has won the Ryan/Kinsella poetry prize, the "Other" Prize, and the Whitechapel Journal short fiction prize. Her short fiction has been published in four anthologies. Her poetry has been published in numerous places, including *HQ Quarterly, The Midwest Coast Review* and *Yes Poetry.*

MARY BAST is a psychologist, life coach, and book coach whose poetry and memoir publications include *Bacopa Literary Review, Connotation Press, Danse Macabre, Dicey Brown, key-ku, Numinous, Rivers, Shaking Like a Mountain, Slow Trains, Tall Grass, The Feathered Founder* and *Wicked Alice.*

NATHALIE BOISARD-BEUDIN is a middle-aged French woman living in Rome, Italy. She has more hobbies than spare time, alas - reading, cooking, writing, painting and photography - so hopes that her technical colleagues at the European Space Agency will soon come up with a solution to that problem by stretching the fabric of time. Either that or send her up to write about the travels and trials of the International Space Station, the way this was done for the exploratory missions of old. Clearly, the woman is a dreamer.

JOHN PAUL CALAVITTA received his MFA from the University of Washington, where he is currently finishing his PhD in English and poetry. His current project is constructing poems from the first lines of poems from the 19th century.

CHRIS CANNELLA is a librarian pursuing an MFA in poetry from the University of Miami. His chapbook, *Suddenly, Nobody*, was published in 2008 by BrickHouse Books, Inc. He is currently working on a collection of historical poems about the Second Seminole War.

MARIA COHUT is a young writer with a degree in English Literature and Creative Writing from the University of Warwick. Bits and bobs of her writing have found their way into online publications such as *Danse Macabre, Subliminal Interiors* and the *Haiku Journal*. She is currently indulging her academic fascination with eighteenth- and nineteenth-century literature, and when she isn't working on one of her projects, she likes to rummage the net and local second-hand bookstores for all things obscure and forgotten.

ANGELA CROFT spent her childhood divided between London, Wales and Cornwall. She worked as a journalist and has been published in a wide range of poetry magazines and on-line and highly commended in a number of competitions including *Aesthetica Creative Writing Annual*, *MsLexia* magazine for her poem on motherhood and *Poetry News* for her response to the anatomical drawings by Leonardo da Vinci.

DEBORAH DUNGAN lives in Santa Fe where she works for the New Mexico Supreme Court. In addition to her law degree, she also holds masters' degrees in child development and grief and loss counseling. She writes creatively as a practice in paying attention.

DAVID ELZEY is a transplanted Californian living in Boston with his heart in Amsterdam. They say past is prologue; he's a former public school teacher, theatre manager, radio DJ, and bookseller who dreamed as a kid he'd grow up to be a swimming pool builder.

DEBORAH HAUSER is the author of *Ennui: From the Diagnostic and Statistical Field Guide of Feminine Disorders* (Finishing Line Press, 2011). She received a Masters in English Literature from Stony Brook University and has taught at Stony Brook University and Suffolk County Community College. Her poetry has been published in numerous print and online journals and anthologies. She lives on Long Island and can be contacted at http://deborahhauser.com.

PAUL HOSTOVSKY is the author of three books of poetry and seven poetry chapbooks. His poems have won a Pushcart Prize and been featured on Poetry Daily, Verse Daily, The Writer's Almanac, and Best of the Net 2008 and 2009. Website: www.paulhostovsky.com.

DANIELLE JONES-PRUETT holds an MFA from the University of Massachusetts Boston. Her work has appeared or is forthcoming in *DMQ Review, Midway Journal, Cider Press Review* and others. She recently purchased a hundred year old house in Salem, and when her husband took down the wallpaper there were found poems all over the walls.

ANGELA KIRBY is a writer and graphic designer located in Raleigh, NC, and the two-time recipient of the Anne-Flexner Prize for Creative Writing at Duke University. Her poems have been published or are forthcoming in *Delirious Hem,* and *Another & Another: An Anthology from the Grind Daily Writing Series* from Bull City Press.

ANDREA M. LOCKETT is a poet, writer, editor, lyricist, yoga teacher, and wine wonk in New York City. She is an associate editor at *The New York Quarterly* magazine, and a co-founder/co-director of The New York Late-Starters String Orchestra (NYLSO). Her first book of poetry will be published in 2013.

DOUGLAS WILLIAM GARCIA MOWBRAY was born in Baltimore, late 70s. Too young for disco. Too old for New Kids on the Block. Early influences include: the neighbor's oldest daughter, 2 Live Crew and Rickey Henderson. Traded baseball players for poets, mid-90s. Current influences: Basho, clogged sewer grates, headless Argentineans standing in crosswalks in the rain with closed umbrellas tapping the white paint of the crosswalks. He is the proprietor of *twentythreebooks*, editor of the *Free Poetry For* chapbook series (http://freepoetryfor.blogspot.com/), and co-founder of *Poetry in Community.*

JOYCE PESEROFF's work has recently appeared in *Memorious, Ploughshares, White Whale Review* and on the Academy of American Poets website.

WINSTON PLOWES is a poet from Hebden Bridge, West Yorkshire, England. He is interested in words of all descriptions and experimental thought processes. Poems he has found have been published recently in *Monkey Kettle, Ink Sweat and Tears, Streetcake, Turbulence* and *Verbatim*. He likes real ale and bicycles. Find out more on his website www.winstonplowes.co.uk.

MARGO ROBY lives and writes poetry in Atlanta, where her husband teaches, so she may continue to do so.

JENNIFER SAUNDERS lives in Switzerland with her Swiss husband and their two Swiss-American sons. She writes poems, struggles with Swiss-German, and teaches small children how to play hockey. Her work has appeared previously in *Found Poetry Review* as well as in *BluePrintReview, Ibbetson Street Magazine, Literary Bohemian, Shot Glass Journal, Classified: An Anthology of Prose Poems* and elsewhere.

KRISTEN SHAW attended Macalester College, where she received the Academy of American Poets Prize. She is now a student at the University of Washington.

MONICA WENDEL is the author of *No Apocalypse* (forthcoming from Georgetown Review Press) and will be the spring 2013 Kerouac Writer in Residence through the Jack Kerouac Project of Orlando, Florida. Her chapbook, *Call it a Window*, was published by the Midwest Writing Center Press in 2012, and her poems have appeared in the *Bellevue Literary Review, Spoon River Poetry Review, Nimrod, Drunken Boat, Forklift, Ohio*, and other journals. A graduate of NYU's MFA in Creative Writing Program, she was the recipient of both Goldwater and Starworks teaching fellowships, and has taught writing to children and adults at Goldwater Hospital, St. Mary's Health Care Center for Kids, NYU, and St. Thomas Aquinas College. She lives in Brooklyn.

Made in the USA
Charleston, SC
16 October 2012